THE INDIAN FOLKTALES

AN EXPLORATION OF INDIA'S ORAL FOLKLORE TRADITIONS

DR. JAGADEESH PILLAI

|| Dedicated to all wisdom seekers around the World ||

ॐ

Contents

Contents

Prayer

"Om Bhadram Karnebhih Shrunuyaama DevaahBhadram Pashyemaakshabhiryajatraah SthirairangaistushtuvaamsastanoobhihVyashema Devahitam YadaayuhSwasti Na Indro VridhashravaahSwasti Nah Pooshaa VishwavedaahSwasti Nastaarkshyo ArishtanemihSwasti No Brihaspatir DadhaatuOm Shantih, Shantih, Shantih"

The literal meaning of this mantra is: OM. O Gods! Let us hear auspicious words from our ears. O reverent Gods! Let us behold propitious visions from our eyes, let our organs and body be stable, healthy, and strong. Let us do that which is pleasing to the gods in the life span allotted to us. May Indra, inscribed in the scriptures, bring us fortune! May Pushan, the knower of the world, grant us prosperity! May Trakshya, who vanquishes enemies, bestow us with blessings! May Brihaspati bring us success!
OM Peace, Peace, Peace.

About the Author

Dr. Jagadeesh Pillai is a renowned Guinness World Record holder, writer, and researcher hailing from Varanasi, also known as the abode of Lord Shiva. With a Ph.D. in Vedic Science and a range of creative ideas and achievements, he is a true polymath. He is the author of more than 100 books including Research Publications. Although his roots can be traced back to Kerala, the people of Varanasi hold him in high regard and affectionately consider him one of their own.

In 1998, Dr. Pillai was offered a job at Banaras Hindu University, but he left the position after only two months to pursue greater goals in life. He believed that in order to study Indian scriptures and engage in other creative endeavours, he needed to retire from the daily grind of working solely for money at a young age.

He started an export business from scratch, using the knowledge he had gained from a previous job in the industry. His intelligence and unique approach to business led to great success in a short period of time, earning him more in just a decade and a half than he would have in a lifetime working in a government job. Upon the passing of Dr. APJ Abdul Kalam, Dr. Pillai decided to leave the business and dedicate himself to reading, studying, researching, and experimenting.

During his tenure in the export business, Dr. Pillai traveled to over 16 countries, gaining valuable insight and experiencing the world and life in detail.

Dr. Pillai has achieved four Guinness World Records in the following subjects:

"Script to Screen" - In this record, Dr. Pillai produced and directed an animation film within the shortest time possible, breaking the previous record set by Canadians. He has also received numerous national and international awards and recognitions for this achievement.

Longest Line of Postcards - For this record, Dr. Pillai created a line of 16,300 postcards on the occasion of the 163rd anniversary of Indian Postal Day. The event also included a questionnaire about the Indian flag.

Largest Poster Awareness Campaign - Dr. Pillai designed an awareness campaign on the subject of "Beti Bachao - Beti Padhao" (Save the Girl Child - Educate the Girl Child) to achieve this record.

Largest Envelope - In tribute to the Indian Prime Minister's "Make in India" initiative, Dr. Pillai created a 4000 square meter envelope using waste paper to achieve this record.

Attempted - **70000 Candles on a 210 kg Cake** - To celebrate the 70th Indian Independence Day, Dr. Pillai attempted to light 70,000 candles on a 210 kg cake, which was recorded in World Records India.

Attempted - **Documentary on Dhamek Stupa of Sarnath in 17 Languages** - Dr. Pillai attempted to create a documentary on the Dhamek Stupa of Sarnath, dubbing it in 17 different languages. The result of this attempt is currently awaiting confirmation from the Guinness World Records.

Dr. Pillai is skilled in teaching the Bhagavad Gita, a Hindu scripture, and is popular among young people. He has helped many young people improve their lives through his motivational teachings.

In addition to teaching, he has composed and sung numerous Sanskrit Bhajans and patriotic songs.

He has also written and directed several short films and documentaries for awareness campaigns, and has volunteered with the police in both UP and Kerala to spread awareness about various issues through videos and photography.

Incredibly, he has produced and directed over 100 documentaries about the city of Varanasi, all on his own.

He has also helped and guided more than 25 boys and girls to achieve world records through creative and innovative methods. He is a multifaceted person who uses his intellect and the blessings given to him by God to excel in various areas. He is both a teacher and a student, always learning and teaching, and is able to master any subject he comes across.

He is a selfless social activist and motivational speaker who has overcome struggles and failures to become a successful and enthusiastic individual with a rich life experience.

In addition to his work with the Bhagavad Gita, he is also an efficient Tarot card reader, Astro-Vastu consultant, and a talented singer and composer. He has sung the entire Ram Charita Manas and Bhagavad Gita in his own compositions, and has sung the phrase "Lokah Samastha Sukhino Bhavantu" in 50 different languages. He is currently working on a detailed and scientific study of Vedas, Upanishads, Puranas, and the Bhagavad Gita. He has also composed and sung the Hanuman Chalisa and Gayatri Mantra in 108 and 1008 different compositions, respectively.

Awards - Four Times Guinness World Records, Winner of Mahatma Gandhi Vishwa Shanti Puraskar, Mahatma Gandhi Global Peace Ambassador, Kashi Ratna Award, Dr. APJ Abdul Kalam Motivational Person of the Year 2017, Mother Teresa Award, Indira Gandhi Priyadarshini Award, Bharat Vikas Ratna Award, Udyog Ratna Award, Vigyan Prasar Award, Poorvanchal Ratn Samman.

PREFACE

Folktales have been an important part of Indian culture since ancient times. These tales, which are passed down orally from generation to generation, provide a window into the culture and history of India. This book, The Indian Folktales: An Exploration of India's Oral Folklore Traditions, seeks to explore the history and significance of Indian folktales and the many ways in which they have shaped Indian culture and society.

This book is intended to serve as an introduction to the rich history and culture of Indian folktales for readers who are new to the subject. It explores the various traditional forms of Indian oral folklore, the role of folktales in Indian culture, and the various types of folktale characters. It also examines the impact of Indian folktales on the global market, the economics of Indian folklore, and the cultural significance of Indian folklore.

The book draws on research from a variety of sources, including interviews with key figures in the Indian folklore industry, archival materials, and cultural analysis. I have also conducted extensive field research in India, including attending storytelling events, interviewing folklorists, and visiting locations associated with the production of Indian folktales. Through this research, I hope to provide readers with a comprehensive understanding of the Indian folktale industry and its various components.

I am deeply passionate about the art of Indian folktales and hope that this book will help to spread the appreciation of this wonderful form of storytelling. I believe that Indian folktales have a great deal to offer to the world and I am excited to share their cultural and historical significance with my readers.

I

Introduction to Indian Folktales

India has a rich and diverse cultural heritage that has been passed down through generations in the form of oral folklore traditions. These traditions have been instrumental in preserving the country's cultural identity and history. Indian folktales are an important part of this rich heritage, embodying the beliefs, values, and customs of the Indian people.

The history of Indian folktales can be traced back to ancient times, with evidence of storytelling in various forms dating back to the Vedic period. These stories were originally passed down orally from one generation to another and were later written down in various texts, such as the Puranas and the Ramayana. Over time, these stories have evolved, with different regions and communities adding their own unique elements to the tales.

Indian folktales are characterized by their imaginative and captivating themes, which often reflect the beliefs and values of the people. These stories are a combination of mythology, legends, and folk beliefs, and they cover a wide range of subjects, including romance, adventure, moral lessons, and supernatural elements. The stories often feature a mix of human and animal characters, and they often revolve around the adventures and misadventures of these characters.

One of the most distinctive features of Indian folktales is their use of symbolism and allegory. The stories often use vivid imagery and allegories to convey moral lessons and wisdom, which has made them an important tool for teaching values and lessons to future generations. The stories also often feature supernatural elements, such as gods and goddesses, demons, and magic, which add to their imaginative and captivating nature.

Indian folktales are also deeply rooted in the country's cultural and social heritage. The stories often reflect the customs and traditions of different regions and communities, and they serve as a means of preserving the cultural heritage of the Indian people. In many cases, these stories have been passed down through generations and have become an integral part of the cultural identity of different communities.

Indian folktales are an important part of the country's rich cultural heritage. These imaginative and captivating stories embody the beliefs, values, and customs of the Indian people, and they have played a significant role in preserving the country's cultural identity and history. They serve as a means of passing down moral lessons and wisdom from one generation to another, and they are an important tool for teaching values and lessons to future generations.

*"Folktales are the whispers of a culture,
telling us the stories that define who we are."*

൹

II

Traditional Forms of Indian Oral Folklore

Traditional Forms of Indian Oral Folklore

Indian oral folklore has taken various forms throughout the country's rich history. From religious stories to secular tales, the storytelling traditions of India have been a part of the cultural fabric for centuries. These traditions have evolved over time, with different regions and communities adding their own unique elements to the tales. In this chapter, we will explore some of the most traditional forms of Indian oral folklore.

Tales of the Puranas

The Puranas are a collection of ancient Hindu religious texts that contain a wealth of mythology, legends, and folklore. These texts were originally passed down orally, and they serve as an important source of information on the beliefs and values of ancient Hindu society. The tales in the Puranas cover a wide range of subjects, including the creation of the universe, the adventures of gods and goddesses, and the history of the world.

Epic Poems

Epic poems, such as the Ramayana and the Mahabharata, are some of the most well-known forms of Indian oral folklore. These epic poems are often written in verse form and tell the stories of great heroes, gods, and goddesses. The Ramayana, for example, tells the story of the prince Rama and his wife Sita, and their quest to defeat the demon king Ravana. The Mahabharata, on the other hand, is a longer epic poem that covers a wide range of subjects, including the history of the world, the adventures of great heroes, and the morality of war.

Folktales

Folktales are a type of storytelling that originated in rural communities and were passed down orally from generation to generation. These tales often feature animal characters and revolve around the adventures and misadventures of these characters. Folktales are a rich source of cultural and moral values, and they often use vivid imagery and allegories to convey moral lessons and wisdom.

Oral Narratives

Oral narratives are a form of storytelling that is performed live, often in front of an audience. These stories are characterized by their improvisational nature, with the storyteller often adapting the story to suit the audience and the situation. Oral narratives can take various forms, including ballads, songs, and epic poems, and they are often used to pass down cultural values and beliefs.

Local Legends

Local legends are stories that are specific to a particular region or community. These legends often revolve around the history and culture of the community, and they often feature local heroes and mythical creatures. Local legends serve as an important means of preserving the cultural heritage of the community and passing down the beliefs and values of the community from generation to generation.

Indian oral folklore has taken various forms throughout the country's rich history. From religious tales to secular stories, these traditions have been instrumental in preserving the cultural heritage and beliefs of the Indian people. Whether in the form of epic poems, folktales, oral narratives, or local legends, these stories continue to captivate audiences of all ages and serve as an important means of passing down cultural values and beliefs from one generation to another.

"*Indian folklore is the soul of the country, a
treasure trove of tradition and heritage.*"

೮೦

III

The Role of Folktales in Indian Culture

The Role of Folktales in Indian Culture

Folktales have played a significant role in Indian culture for centuries. From entertaining and educating children to preserving cultural heritage and values, these stories have served a variety of purposes throughout India's rich history. In this chapter, we will explore the role that folktales have played in Indian culture, and how they continue to influence and shape the country's cultural landscape.

Education and Moral Instruction

One of the most important roles that folktales have played in Indian culture is that of education and moral instruction. Many folktales feature animal characters and revolve around the adventures and misadventures of these characters. These tales often use vivid imagery and allegories to convey moral lessons and wisdom, and they serve as an effective means of teaching children about right and wrong. By using humor, vivid imagery, and memorable characters, folktales have been able to engage and educate young people, helping them to internalize important cultural values and beliefs.

Preserving Cultural Heritage

Another important role that folktales have played in Indian culture is that of preserving cultural heritage. As communities and regions change over time, folktales serve as an important means of preserving the cultural heritage of the community and passing down the beliefs and values of the community from generation to generation. By preserving the cultural heritage of the community, folktales help to maintain a sense of continuity and identity, and they provide a connection to the community's past.

Entertaining and Engaging

Folktales have also played a significant role in Indian culture as a source of entertainment. The vivid imagery, memorable characters, and engaging stories of folktales have captivated audiences of all ages, providing a source of entertainment and distraction from the daily routine. By entertaining and engaging audiences, folktales have helped to bring people together, fostering a sense of community and shared experience.

Reflection of Society and Values

Folktales also serve as a reflection of the values and beliefs of the society in which they are told. These stories often reflect the moral and cultural values of the community, as well as the social and political norms of the time. By examining the content and themes of folktales, it is possible to gain insight into the beliefs and values of the society that produced them. This makes folktales an important tool for understanding the cultural heritage and beliefs of a community.

Influence on Literature and Art

Finally, folktales have also played a significant role in the development of Indian literature and art. Many writers and artists have been inspired by the stories and characters of folktales, incorporating them into their own works. This has helped to preserve the cultural heritage of the folktales and has ensured that these stories will continue to be a part of the cultural landscape for generations to come.

Folktales have played a significant role in Indian culture for centuries. From entertaining and educating children to preserving cultural heritage and values, these stories have served a variety of purposes and have influenced and shaped the country's cultural landscape in numerous ways. Whether as a source of entertainment, education, or reflection of society and values, folktales continue to captivate audiences and serve as an important means of preserving the cultural heritage of the Indian people.

*"In the telling of a folktale, we bring to life
the essence of our culture."*

౩౨

IV
Types of Indian Folktale Characters

Indian folktales are rich in their use of diverse and memorable characters, each with their own unique personalities, motivations, and stories. In this chapter, we will explore the different types of characters that are commonly found in Indian folktales and examine the role they play in these stories.

Animals

One of the most common types of characters in Indian folktales are animals. These animal characters are often depicted as anthropomorphic, possessing human-like qualities and abilities. From the clever jackal to the brave lion, animal characters in Indian folktales serve as allegories for human traits and behaviors, offering lessons and wisdom through their adventures and misadventures. The use of animal characters in these tales helps to make the stories more accessible and memorable, as well as helping to impart important moral lessons in a way that is easily understood.

Gods and Goddesses

Another type of character that is commonly found in Indian folktales are gods and goddesses. These characters often play important roles in the tales, serving as powerful and benevolent forces that help to shape the world and the lives of the characters within it. Gods and goddesses in Indian folktales are often depicted as powerful, wise, and compassionate, helping to guide and protect the other characters in their stories. These divine characters also serve as a means of exploring and expressing the cultural beliefs and values of the society in which the tales are told.

Demons and Monsters

Along with gods and goddesses, demons and monsters are also a common type of character found in Indian folktales. These characters often serve as obstacles or antagonists, challenging the heroes of the tales and serving as a means of exploring the darker side of human nature. Demons and monsters in Indian folktales are often depicted as cruel, manipulative, and dangerous, representing the forces of evil in the world. The struggles of the heroes against these evil forces help to impart important moral lessons, such as the importance of bravery, courage, and determination.

Heroes and Heroines

The heroes and heroines of Indian folktales are often the

central characters of these tales, facing challenges and overcoming obstacles as they strive to achieve their goals. These characters are depicted as brave, resourceful, and virtuous, serving as examples of the best qualities of human nature. The heroes and heroines of Indian folktales help to impart important moral lessons and serve as a source of inspiration, encouraging others to strive for the same qualities of bravery, courage, and determination.

Tricksters

Tricksters are another type of character that is commonly found in Indian folktales. These characters are often depicted as cunning, clever, and mischievous, using their wit and cunning to get what they want. Although tricksters are often depicted as selfish and unprincipled, they also serve a larger purpose in the tales, helping to challenge the status quo and encouraging others to think creatively and critically. The antics of the tricksters in these tales often help to bring humor and lightheartedness to the stories, making them more entertaining and engaging.

Indian folktales are rich in their use of diverse and memorable characters, each with their own unique personalities, motivations, and stories. Whether depicted as gods and goddesses, heroes and heroines, demons and monsters, animals, or tricksters, these characters serve as a means of exploring the human condition and imparting important moral lessons. The variety of characters found in Indian folktales helps to make these stories more engaging, entertaining, and memorable, ensuring that they will continue to be an important part of India's cultural heritage for generations to come.

"Folktales are not just stories, they are a window into the heart and soul of a people."

‽

V

Popular Indian Folktale Genres

Indian folktales are diverse and rich in their use of different genres, each with their own unique themes, characters, and storytelling styles. In this chapter, we will explore some of the most popular genres of Indian folktales, examining the characteristics and themes that define each genre and how they contribute to the overall cultural heritage of India.

Jataka Tales

Jataka tales are a type of Buddhist folktale that originated in India and have since spread throughout Southeast Asia. These tales are often centered around the previous lives of the Buddha, known as the Jataka tales, and are used to impart moral lessons and wisdom. Jataka tales are characterized by their use of anthropomorphic animal characters, and often involve complex narratives filled with allegories and symbolic imagery. These tales serve as an important part of Buddhist tradition, helping to promote moral values and encouraging reflection on the Buddhist teachings.

Panchatantra Tales

The Panchatantra is a collection of Indian folktales that are believed to have been written in Sanskrit as early as the 3rd century BCE. These tales are characterized by their use of animals as the main characters, and are often framed as a series of moral lessons and fables. The Panchatantra tales are known for their clever use of wit and humor, as well as their ability to impart important lessons and wisdom. These tales are still widely popular in India today, and have been translated into numerous languages, making them an important part of the cultural heritage of India.

Puranic Tales

Puranic tales are a genre of Hindu folktales that are centered around the gods and goddesses of Hinduism. These tales are often used to explore the Hindu mythology and traditions, and are characterized by their use of divine characters and supernatural events. Puranic tales often involve complex narratives and epic adventures, and are often used to impart moral lessons and wisdom. These tales are an important part of Hindu tradition, and serve as a means of exploring the cultural beliefs and values of Hinduism.

Ramayana and Mahabharata Tales

The Ramayana and the Mahabharata are two of the most

famous epic poems in Indian literature. These tales are characterized by their use of grand and heroic characters, and are often centered around the adventures and struggles of the gods and heroes of Hindu mythology. The Ramayana and the Mahabharata are often used to explore important themes such as love, loyalty, courage, and determination, and are an important part of Hindu tradition. These tales have been widely passed down from generation to generation, and remain an important part of India's cultural heritage.

Sufi Tales

Sufi tales are a genre of folktales that originated in the Islamic Sufi tradition and have since spread throughout the Middle East and South Asia. These tales are characterized by their use of allegory and symbolic imagery, and are often used to explore important spiritual and moral themes. Sufi tales often feature wise and learned characters who use their wit and wisdom to impart lessons and wisdom to others. These tales are an important part of the Islamic Sufi tradition, and serve as a means of exploring the cultural beliefs and values of this tradition.

Indian folktales are diverse and rich in their use of different genres, each with their own unique themes, characters, and storytelling styles. Whether exploring Buddhist teachings, Hindu mythology, or Islamic spiritual values, these tales serve as an important part of India's cultural heritage, helping to promote moral values, impart important lessons and wisdom, and explore the cultural beliefs and values of India's many different traditions.

ॐ

*"The tradition of oral storytelling in India is
a testament to the power of the human voice."*

ॐ

VI

The Impact of Indian Folktales on Society

Indian folktales have played an important role in shaping and reflecting the cultural beliefs, values, and traditions of Indian society for thousands of years. From imparting moral lessons and wisdom, to exploring the complex relationships between different groups and individuals, these tales have helped to shape the cultural identity of India and its people.

Shaping Cultural Values and Beliefs

Indian folktales have played an important role in shaping the cultural values and beliefs of India, serving as a means of transmitting important moral lessons and wisdom from one generation to the next. These tales often feature characters and events that embody important cultural values such as courage, honesty, and respect, and help to reinforce these values in the minds of listeners. In this way, Indian folktales serve as a means of preserving cultural heritage and transmitting important cultural values to future generations.

Reflecting Social Relationships

Indian folktales often reflect the complex relationships and dynamics that exist within Indian society. These tales often explore the relationships between different groups, such as different castes or religious communities, as well as the relationships between individuals and their families. Through these tales, listeners can gain a deeper understanding of the social relationships and dynamics that exist within their communities, and can learn about the importance of empathy, compassion, and understanding.

Promoting Understanding and Tolerance

Indian folktales often feature characters from diverse backgrounds and cultures, and serve as a means of promoting understanding and tolerance between different groups. By exploring the relationships and interactions between different characters, these tales help to break down cultural barriers and promote empathy and compassion between different groups. In this way, Indian folktales play an important role in promoting social harmony and encouraging understanding and tolerance between different cultures and communities.

Providing a Platform for Social and Political Commentary

Indian folktales often provide a platform for social and political commentary, exploring important themes and issues that are relevant to Indian society. Through their use of allegory and symbolic imagery, these tales provide a means of addressing sensitive social and political issues in a way that is both nuanced and powerful. In this way, Indian folktales play an important role in shaping the cultural discourse and providing a platform for social and political commentary.

Celebrating Cultural Diversity

Indian folktales are diverse and reflect the rich cultural heritage of India. From the Jataka tales of Buddhism, to the Puranic tales of Hinduism, to the Sufi tales of Islam, these tales celebrate the cultural diversity of India and help to reinforce the cultural heritage of its many different communities and traditions. Through their celebration of cultural diversity, Indian folktales help to promote social harmony and reinforce the cultural heritage of India.

Indian folktales have had a profound impact on Indian society, playing an important role in shaping cultural values and beliefs, reflecting social relationships, promoting understanding and tolerance, providing a platform for social and political commentary, and celebrating cultural diversity. These tales serve as an important part of India's cultural heritage, helping to preserve its cultural traditions and imparting important moral lessons and wisdom to future generations.

౭౨

*"Folktales hold within them the wisdom of
the ages, passed down through generations."*

୬

VII

The Economics of
Indian Folklore

The production and dissemination of Indian folktales has been an important source of income for many communities in India for generations. In addition to their cultural and social value, these tales have also played an important economic role in Indian society, providing a means of livelihood for storytellers, artists, and other professionals involved in their production and dissemination.

Storytelling as a Profession

In many parts of India, storytelling has been a traditional profession, with professional storytellers traveling from village to village, entertaining audiences with their tales. These storytellers were often paid a fee for their performances, which provided them with a source of livelihood. In addition, many storytellers were also able to supplement their income by selling copies of their tales in the form of books or manuscripts.

The Production of Folktale-related Products

In addition to the production and dissemination of folktales themselves, the production of folktale-related products such as books, paintings, sculptures, and musical recordings has also been an important source of income for many communities in India. For example, the production of illustrated books featuring Indian folktales has been an important source of income for artists and illustrators, while the production of musical recordings has provided a source of income for musicians and other performers.

The Tourism Industry

The rich cultural heritage of India, including its folklore traditions, has also been an important factor in the growth of the tourism industry in India. Many tourists visit India each year specifically to learn about its folklore traditions and to experience its cultural heritage firsthand. This has provided an important source of income for many communities in India, as well as boosting the local economy by generating revenue through the sale of goods and services related to tourism.

The Film and Entertainment Industry

The rich cultural heritage of India, including its folklore traditions, has also been an important factor in the growth of the film and entertainment industry in India. Many Indian films and television programs are based on folktales, providing a source of income for writers, directors, actors, and other professionals involved in the production of these works. In addition, the production of these works has also helped to raise awareness of Indian folklore traditions and has provided a source of income for communities that are involved in the production of these works.

The Publishing Industry

The publication and dissemination of Indian folktales in the form of books has also been an important source of income for many communities in India. The sale of books featuring Indian folktales has provided a source of income for publishers, writers, and other professionals involved in the production and dissemination of these works. In addition, the sale of these books has helped to raise awareness of Indian folklore traditions and has provided a source of income for communities that are involved in their production and dissemination.

Indian folklore has played an important economic role in Indian society, providing a source of income for many communities through the production and dissemination of tales, folktale-related products, and related industries such as tourism, film and entertainment, and publishing. These economic benefits have helped to preserve and promote India's rich cultural heritage, while also providing a source of livelihood for those involved in its production and dissemination.

*"Indian folklore is a rich tapestry of tales
that reflect the diversity and complexity of
the country."*

৪৩

VIII

The Cultural Significance of Indian Folklore

Indian folklore holds a significant place in the country's rich cultural heritage and has played an important role in shaping its cultural identity. The tales, legends, songs, and other forms of oral tradition that make up Indian folklore provide a window into the beliefs, values, and traditions of the country's diverse communities. They also offer valuable insights into the social and cultural history of India, providing a rich and complex picture of the country's past.

Reflection of Cultural Diversity

One of the most notable aspects of Indian folklore is its diversity, reflecting the rich cultural tapestry of India's many communities. From the remote mountain regions of the north to the coastal plains of the south, Indian folklore is rich in tales, legends, and songs that are unique to each region and each community. This diversity reflects the country's cultural, linguistic, and ethnic diversity, and provides a valuable resource for learning about the cultural heritage of India's many communities.

Insights into Cultural Beliefs and Values

Indian folklore is also an important source of insight into the cultural beliefs and values of India's many communities. The tales and legends of Indian folklore often feature traditional cultural heroes, gods, and other supernatural beings, providing a rich picture of the cultural beliefs and values of the communities that created them. These tales also often reflect the social, political, and economic realities of the time, offering valuable insights into the cultural history of India's many communities.

Preservation of Cultural Heritage

Indian folklore has also played an important role in preserving the cultural heritage of the country's many communities. These tales, legends, songs, and other forms of oral tradition have been passed down from generation to generation, providing a valuable resource for learning about the cultural heritage of India's many communities. In addition, the continued production and dissemination of Indian folklore has helped to preserve and promote the cultural heritage of the country, while also providing a source of livelihood for those involved in its production and dissemination.

Education and Socialization

Indian folklore also plays an important role in the education and socialization of children in India. Tales and legends are often used as a way of teaching children about cultural values and beliefs, and of imparting important lessons about life and morality. These tales also provide children with a window into the cultural heritage of their communities, helping to foster a sense of pride and connection to their cultural roots.

Cultural Identity

Finally, Indian folklore is also an important aspect of the cultural identity of the country's many communities. The tales, legends, and other forms of oral tradition that make up Indian folklore provide a rich and complex picture of the cultural heritage of India's many communities, and help to define their cultural identities. By preserving and promoting this cultural heritage, Indian folklore helps to maintain the cultural identities of the country's many communities, while also fostering a sense of pride and connection to their cultural roots.

Indian folklore holds a significant place in the country's rich cultural heritage, reflecting the cultural, linguistic, and ethnic diversity of India's many communities. It provides valuable insights into the cultural beliefs and values of India's many communities, and has played an important role in preserving and promoting the cultural heritage of the country. Through its role in education and socialization, Indian folklore also helps to define the cultural identities of the country's many communities, while fostering a sense of pride and connection to their cultural roots.

"Folktales are not just for children, they are for anyone who wants to understand the world and their place in it."

൙

IX

Preservation of Indian Folklore

Indian folklore, like any other traditional form of oral storytelling, has been passed down from generation to generation through verbal means. With the advent of technology and globalization, it has become increasingly important to preserve this rich heritage of stories, songs, and other forms of folklore. The preservation of Indian folklore is crucial to ensure that these traditional tales remain a significant part of Indian culture and remain accessible to future generations.

One way to preserve Indian folklore is through the written word. Many of the most famous folktales from India have been recorded and translated into written form, making them accessible to a wider audience. This has not only helped to preserve the stories themselves, but also to preserve the cultural and linguistic diversity of India. The oral tradition of Indian folklore can also be preserved through audio recordings, which can capture the nuances of storytelling and the rich cultural heritage that is embodied in these tales.

Another important aspect of preserving Indian folklore is to keep the oral tradition alive. This can be done by encouraging the sharing of folktales among communities, schools, and families. This not only keeps the tradition alive, but also helps to preserve the cultural values and beliefs that are embodied in the stories. For example, the moral lessons that are woven into many Indian folktales can help to shape the attitudes and values of those who listen to them, and can be an important tool for transmitting cultural knowledge and wisdom.

In addition to preserving the oral tradition, it is also important to promote the study and appreciation of Indian folklore. This can be done through academic research, cultural events, and festivals that celebrate the richness and diversity of Indian folklore. By encouraging the study of Indian folklore, we can not only help to preserve these tales, but also gain a deeper understanding of the cultural and historical context in which they were created.

The digital age has also brought new opportunities for preserving Indian folklore. Online platforms, such as digital archives and websites, have made it possible to access a vast collection of folktales from India and other parts of the world. This has not only made it easier to preserve these stories, but also to share them with a wider audience, helping to promote cultural exchange and understanding.

Preserving Indian folklore is crucial to ensure that these rich and diverse tales remain an important part of Indian culture for generations to come. By promoting the sharing and study of these tales, and by using the latest technology and resources to preserve the oral tradition, we can help to ensure that the cultural significance of Indian folklore remains intact. Whether through written records, audio recordings, or digital archives, the preservation of Indian folklore is an important aspect of preserving the cultural heritage of India and ensuring that these tales remain accessible to future generations.

"The preservation of Indian folklore is a duty
we owe to future generations, to ensure that
these traditions continue to thrive."

ജ

X

Indian Folktales and the Global Market

Indian folktales have become an important part of the global market, with an increasing number of books, movies, and other media products being created and marketed based on these tales. This has had a profound impact on the way that Indian folklore is perceived and valued both within India and around the world.

One of the ways that Indian folktales have become a part of the global market is through the publication of children's books. Many classic Indian folktales, such as "The Panchatantra" and "The Ramayana," have been translated and adapted for children, and are now widely available in many different languages. This has helped to introduce Indian folklore to a new generation of readers and to promote cultural exchange between India and the rest of the world.

The film industry has also played a significant role in promoting Indian folktales on the global market. Bollywood, the Indian film industry, has produced a number of movies based on classic Indian folktales, including "Ramayana: The Epic" and "Sivaji." These movies have helped to popularize Indian folklore and to promote a deeper understanding of the cultural and historical context in which these tales were created.

In addition to traditional media products, the internet has also played a significant role in promoting Indian folktales on the global market. Online platforms, such as websites and social media, have made it easier for people around the world to access and share information about Indian folklore. This has created new opportunities for the promotion and marketing of Indian folktales, and has helped to raise awareness of these tales among a global audience.

The popularity of Indian folktales has also had an impact on the tourism industry in India. Many tourists are now interested in exploring the rich cultural heritage of India, and are eager to learn more about the country's folktales and other traditional forms of storytelling. This has led to the development of cultural tours and festivals that showcase the diversity and richness of Indian folklore.

The global market for Indian folktales has also created new opportunities for the monetization of these tales. Many folk artists, writers, and other cultural producers are now able to make a living through the creation and sale of products based on Indian folklore. This has helped to promote the value and importance of these tales, and has encouraged the continuation of the oral tradition of storytelling in India.

The global market for Indian folktales has had a profound impact on the way that these tales are perceived and valued. By promoting Indian folklore through books, movies, and other media products, and by making these tales accessible to a wider audience, the global market has helped to preserve and promote this rich cultural heritage. Whether through the publishing industry, the film industry, or the internet, the global market for Indian folktales has helped to promote cultural exchange and understanding, and has created new opportunities for the monetization of these tales.

"Folktales are a connection to our past, and a guide for our future."

৪৩

XI

The Future of Indian Folklore

Indian folklore is an intrinsic part of the country's cultural heritage and has been passed down from generation to generation through oral traditions. With the rapidly changing world, it is important to examine the future of this rich and diverse cultural resource. The future of Indian folklore will be shaped by a variety of factors, including technology, globalization, and the changing social and economic conditions of Indian society.

The role of technology:

In recent years, technology has had a profound impact on the way folktales are shared and preserved. With the advent of the internet and digital media, traditional folktales are now available to a wider audience than ever before. People can now access these stories through websites, mobile apps, and e-books. This has opened up new opportunities for folktale enthusiasts and scholars to learn about, research, and preserve these important cultural treasures.

However, technology also has its drawbacks. As more and more people turn to digital media for entertainment and information, traditional storytelling methods are becoming less popular. This is particularly true among young people, who may find these older forms of storytelling less appealing than more modern forms of entertainment.

Globalization:

Globalization is another factor that will have a significant impact on the future of Indian folklore. With the increasing interconnectedness of the world, cultural exchange and influences are becoming more common. This means that Indian folktales will be exposed to new audiences and will likely be influenced by other cultures and traditions. This can be seen as both a positive and negative development, as it may lead to the preservation of these important cultural resources, but it may also result in the dilution of their unique qualities and significance.

Social and economic changes:

The social and economic changes taking place in India will also play a role in shaping the future of its folklore. As India becomes more urbanized and industrialized, traditional forms of storytelling may become less common and may be replaced by more modern forms of entertainment. This may lead to the decline of traditional storytelling communities and the loss of valuable cultural resources.

In addition, the economic conditions of Indian society will also play a role in shaping the future of its folklore. As more and more people move into urban areas and become economically well-off, they may become less interested in traditional forms of storytelling and more interested in other forms of entertainment. This could lead to a decline in the popularity of folktales and a corresponding decline in the number of people who preserve and pass them down.

Preservation and promotion:

To ensure the future of Indian folklore, it is important to preserve and promote these important cultural resources. This can be done in a number of ways, including:

Encouraging the continuation of traditional storytelling methods and supporting communities that preserve these methods.

Documenting and preserving folktales in written and digital form.

Promoting folktales and their significance through education and media.

Encouraging the use of folktales in contemporary art, literature, and popular culture.

Encouraging the development of new technologies that will help preserve and promote folktales.

Conclusion:

The future of Indian folklore is uncertain, but with the right approach, it can be preserved and promoted for future generations. By recognizing the importance of these cultural resources and taking steps to protect and promote them, we can ensure that they will continue to be a rich and vibrant part of Indian culture for years to come. Whether through technology, globalization, or social and economic changes, the future of Indian folklore is sure to be shaped by a variety of factors. But with the right approach, it can continue to be a valuable and significant part of India's cultural heritage for generations to come, inspiring future generations with its wisdom, beauty, and timeless appeal."

Indian folklore has been a source of rich cultural heritage and has played an important role in shaping the identity of the country. The future of Indian folklore is uncertain as the world becomes more globalized and modern. However, there are several initiatives underway to ensure that these traditions continue to be passed down to future generations.

One way to ensure the preservation of Indian folklore is through education. Many schools and universities in India now offer courses on folklore, which help students understand the cultural significance of these tales. The government has also launched initiatives to promote the study of folklore, which helps to raise awareness and encourage people to take an interest in their cultural heritage.

Another way to preserve Indian folklore is through

technology. With the widespread availability of digital media, traditional stories can now be recorded and shared with a larger audience. This allows the stories to reach new generations, who may not have had access to them otherwise. In addition, technology has enabled the digitization of many Indian folklore collections, which makes it easier for researchers to access and study these tales.

The future of Indian folklore will also be shaped by the role of the media. The media has the ability to shape public opinion and to promote cultural values. The media can be used to bring attention to the importance of Indian folklore and to encourage people to learn about and appreciate these traditions.

Finally, the future of Indian folklore will be influenced by the changing cultural landscape of India. As the country continues to modernize, there is a risk that traditional values and traditions may be lost. However, the preservation of folklore remains an important aspect of cultural identity and it is crucial that people continue to support and preserve these traditions.

Indian folklore is an important part of the country's cultural heritage and has the potential to play a significant role in shaping the future of the country. Through education, technology, the media, and continued support, the future of Indian folklore looks bright and it is likely that these traditions will continue to be passed down from generation to generation.

"Through the exploration of Indian folklore,
we not only learn about the country's rich
cultural heritage, but also about ourselves."

☙

Other Books Of The Author

1. The Moments When I Met God
2. Kashiyile Theertha Pathangal
3. GURU GYAN VANI
4. Abhiprerak Gita
5. ASSI SE JAIN GHAT TAK
6. Hopelessness of Arjuna
7. The Soul and It's True Nature
8. Sense of Action (Karma)
9. Action through Wisdom
10. Action through Wisdom
11. THEORY AND PRACTICAL OF EVERY ACTION
12. LOGICAL UNDERSTANDING OF THE SUPREME
13. THE IMPERISHABLE SUPREME
14. Yatra Nishadraj se Hanuman Ghat Tak
15. Yatra Karnatak Ghat se Raja Ghat Tak
16. Yatra Pandey Ghat se Prayagraj Ghat Tak
17. Yatra Ranjendra Prasad Ghat se Dattatreya Ghat Tak
18. YaatraSindhiya Ghat se Gwaliar Ghat Tak
19. Yatra Mangala Gauri Ghat se Hanuman Gadhi Ghat Tak
20. Yatra Gaay Ghat Se Nishad Ghat Tak
21. MAA GANGA, GHATEN EVM UTSAV
22. Ganga Arti Dev Deepavali evam Any Utsav
23. Potentials of Digitalized India
24. VEDIC CONSCIOUSNESS
25. A Brief Introduction to Vedic Science
26. Kashi ke Barah Jyotirling
27. IMPACT OF MOTIVATION
28. Let's have a Milky Way Journey
29. Color Therapy in a Nutshell

Contacy

DR. JAGADEESH PILLAI

MBA & PhD in Vedic Science

Four Times Guinness World Record Holder

Winner of Mahatma Gandhi Vishwa Shanti Puraskar and
Global Peace Ambassador

Gemology, Astro & Vastu Consultant - Spiritual Counselor

Consultant for designing World Record Ideas

Efficient Tarot Card Reader

9839093003

myrichindia@gmail.com

drjagadeeshpillai@facebook

drjagadeeshpillai@instagram
jagadeeshpillai@youtube

www. JAGADEESHPILLAI.com

|| LOKAHA SAMASTHAHA SUKHINO BHAVANTU ||